PRENTICE-HALL
CONTEMPORARY PERSPECTIVES IN MUSIC EDUCATION SERIES
Charles Leonhard, Editor

PRENTICE-HALL INTERNATIONAL, INC., London
PRENTICE-HALL OF AUSTRALIA, PTY. LTD., Sydney
PRENTICE-HALL OF CANADA, LTD., Toronto
PRENTICE-HALL OF INDIA PRIVATE LTD., New Delhi
PRENTICE-HALL OF JAPAN, INC., Tokyo

experimental research

in music

CLIFFORD K. MADSEN
School of Music, The Florida State University

CHARLES H. MADSEN, JR.
Department of Psychology, The Florida State University

PRENTICE-HALL, INC., Englewood Cliffs, New Jersey

MT
1
.M13
1970
149869
Sept. 1970

Printed in the United States of America

C–13–295097–9
P–13–295089–8

Library of Congress Catalog Card No.: 70–79831

Current Printing (last digit):

10 9 8 7 6 5 4 3 2 1

foreword

Contemporary Perspectives in Music Education is a new series of professional books for music education. It establishes a pattern for music teacher education based on the areas of knowledge and processes involved in music education rather than on the levels and specializations in music education.

The areas of knowledge include philosophy of music education, psychology of music teaching, and research methods. The processes include program development, instruction, administration, supervision, and evaluation.

The basic premise of the series is that mastery of all of these processes and areas of knowledge is essential for the successful music educator regardless of his area of specialization and the level at which he teaches. The series presents in a systematic fashion information and concepts basic to a unified music education profession.

All of the books in the series have been designed and written for use in the undergraduate program of music teacher education. The pattern of the series is both systematic and flexible. It permits music education instructors at the college level to select one or more of the books as texts on the basis of their relevance to a particular course.

In their book, *Experimental Research in Music*, Professor Clifford Madsen and Professor Charles Madsen treat the concepts and techniques basic to experimental research. Their book is remarkable not only for its clarity and comprehensiveness but also for its refreshing and highly readable style.

I shall never forget the occasion of my first reading of this book in manuscript. Having grown accustomed to treatises on research being dull and pedantic, I was amazed and delighted to find myself reading a book on research that was interesting, witty, and down-to-earth, but at the same time filled with information and insights for the beginning researcher in music. There was not the slightest doubt in my mind that this book belonged in Contemporary Perspectives in Music Education.

Music educators are becoming increasingly aware of the necessity for research in music education and the importance of using research and research results in the teaching of music. This book will make a real contribution to a higher level of professionalism in music education which can only be achieved by research oriented teachers of music.

Charles Leonhard

preface

This text is written for advanced undergraduate and graduate students in music who have not had previous instruction in experimental research. Initially, scientific interest is best nurtured by actual experimentation. Therefore, the text is deliberately concise and may be completed concurrently with experimentation. It is written in two parts which may be studied sequentially or by alternating the two sections combining Chapters One and Six, Two and Seven, Three and Eight, Four and Nine, and Five and Ten. The text is primarily intended for a first course in Experimental Research in Music. It may also be used as supplementary reading for courses in Psychology of Music, Music Education, Music Therapy, or Research Methods in Music.

Many musicians recognize the advisability of conducting experimental research but do not know how to get started. The authors contend that students in music should have the opportunity *to begin* experimental research regardless of scientific naivete. In Part One, broad classifications of music topics are presented to stimulate research interest. In Part Two, experimental terminology, rationale, and methodology are introduced. The text is neither a current review of experimentation in music nor a substitute for specific courses in statistics and experimental design. It is the authors' hope that this introduction will provide an impetus for additional experimental research in music.

C.K.M. / C.H.M.

contents

QUESTIONING TRADITION

Music is necessarily a live art, and quality performance continues to prevail. It seems progressively more difficult however, to attract the musical potentialities required for continued artistic excellence. In some instances, the time required to achieve musical finesse seems prohibitive; additionally, many potential performers are lost to other areas.

Musicians basically use traditional approaches that have been passed down through the ages. There are inherent advantages to apprenticeship systems, but they leave little opportunity for speed and efficiency and are definitely out of step with the demands of modern-day instruction. Possibly, the most significant reason for the exclusive perpetuation of these traditional approaches is the conspicuous lack of valid experimental research in applied music. Surprisingly, even though some efforts are being made in this area, some performers seem reluctant to avail themselves of the new ideas and knowledge incorporated in the findings of experimental research. Some performing musicians seem to be unconcerned with anything that cannot be passed on in the privacy of the studio. Many articles, methods, and demonstration-lectures produce little more than personal "testimonials" concerning how music should be performed.

The novice is perplexed and often discouraged in trying to arrive at tangible answers for improving performance skills. A young performer often finds himself in a situation which tacitly demands that he function in an intangible world of pet phrases and unproven suppositions. He is sometimes led to believe that to learn music he must find the right teacher, lose himself in a particular cult, and be implicitly faithful. This student may come to realize that it does not seem to matter how long he has studied or with whom. Each encounter with a new teacher usually demands that, in order to be initiated into the teacher's method, the student substantially reject much of his past learning. The aspiring performer then takes one more step in a never-ending process of tearing down one method in order to replace it with another. If thoughtful, he may realize after many years that for the best performer in the world, the pattern would possibly be the same. The performer might still leave this new teacher's studio with the teacher smiling at him condescendingly saying, "Son, it's good you got here in time. Work hard and do as I say and I will correct all those bad habits, and you will perform correctly."

The tremendous facility required for professional performance demands optimum speed. Much time is wasted when conflicting opinions, which could be tested experimentally, are argued and debated. It would appear that if live musical performance is to continue, other than in highly specialized recording groups, something needs to be done to help parallel in the positive objective thinking that many people use in daily life. For example, the thinking of a student who seriously considers the possibility of death on the highway when traveling hundreds of miles to get home, the thinking that stimulates regular medical attention, or the thinking related to choice of professional occupation. Many who have worked with wayward friends, maladjusted children, or mental patients immediately recognize the *unobjective thinking* that brings many of these people to the therapist's door. A primary concern of therapist, teacher, or friend is to avoid perpetuating the misdirected and misguided thought processes that incapacitate and cause premature death. The research attitude represents an objective view of the world, and the finished product, hopefully, is a person who is informed and has the ability to think, that is, to analyze, to criticize, and to choose alternatives in the light of all possible evidence.

Research is a *modus operandi,* a method by which men can organize actions to be consistent with their thoughts and test these actions intelligently, realizing that through thoughtful trial and error they can better ascertain the worth of their ideas. Most criminal courts evidence tremendous leniency following first offenses, but improved behavior and some understanding about the "hot stove" are assumed after the first "burn."

Research is a manner of evaluation. When making a choice is imperative and action has been taken, the thoughtful person evaluates that action to determine how prior choices affect future eventualities. It does appear strange that even after having been "burned," one often respeats previous mistakes usually assuring similar unfortunate outcomes. Often, there is a misapprehension that if one knows the consequences of an action, he will *not* choose unwisely; but anyone who has received a second traffic ticket, eaten too much every Thanksgiving, or procrastinated studying until the end of every term attests to the fallibility of man. To recognize this fallibility and suspect those desires that clothe themselves in the respectability of thought is perhaps the first step toward the scientific attitude, especially concerning evaluation of previous experiences.

Thus, the research attitude is characterized by three general aspects: (1) an objective state of mind, (2) a structured mode of action, and (3) evaluation for future action. In dealing with the arts, research is sometimes defined very broadly to include creativity and other more subtle aspects not generally associated with objective facts. Regardless, it should be remembered that research does not establish absolutes. It develops explanations and predictions that hold until further investigations provide greater information. Scientific inquiry represents a process toward "truth" relative to man's depth of understanding.

tical and artistic fulfillments of other areas of endeavor have not been nearly so limited by this "either-or" dilemma as have those of music.

THE ART OF MUSIC

The pursuit of aesthetic experiences would appear to be not only the first but also the highest endeavor of which man is capable. It is extremely discouraging to find that those primarily concerned with aesthetic endeavors fail to realize that most scientists share this concern. The scientist is also a dreamer (a Romantic, as it were), whose concern is a more complete actualization of man's potentials.

There are many similarities between the scientist and aesthetician. A scientist starts with a hypothesis, euphemistically, a dream. Over a period of time, he develops and builds upon his hypothesis with a goal toward the beautiful. However, all aspects of scientific endeavor demand a paramount necessity for objectification. The scientist's mode of inquiry is based upon structure and rigorous empirical investigation. It is not that he is unconcerned with beauty. Beauty comes from achieving greater specific knowledge. Beauty resides within stringent methodology. Beauty comes from the excitement of each new discovery. Indeed, ultimate beauty seems identical for both science and aesthetics—those endeavors which represent the optimum of which the entire resourcefulness of man is capable.

THE SCIENTIFIC ATTITUDE

Surprisingly, most musicians have only vague ideas concerning research and the place it could have in the music profession. Many musicians believe that research, although respectable, has no real meaning for anyone except esoteric experimenters who lose themselves in inconspicuous laboratories and experiment with musical effects on everything except those aspects that could really benefit the music profession. This attitude may be partially correct, but it is so limited in describing research that it fails to see most of the important aspects of this potentially powerful endeavor.

Research, in the broadest definition, is a way of thinking, a state of mind. It is an attempt to think rationally and objectively concerning those aspects of life that can be studied scientifically. It is a rigorous discipline that attempts to separate fact from fantasy and to test observations in light of objective evidence. This attitude is not necessarily limited to a controlled experiment, which tests specific variables; it also has a

CHAPTER ONE

music as an art and a science

Many of man's difficulties seem to arise from his naiveté in grouping together aspects of life that are mutually exclusive, and alternately, his inability to distinguish situations and ideas that are necessarily "either-or." [1] Traditionally, most musicians have been in the latter grouping. Even at present, there appears to be a large chasm between musicians interested in more objective approaches to music and those who appear to believe that music as an art would suffer if subjected to scientific scrutiny.

Although this dichotomy is partially justified, it represents an anachronism and may eventually prepare the demise of music as a live art. One need only reflect for a moment on the many accomplishments in the physical and social sciences, as well as on the more commonplace advancements of our present technological age, to realize the limitations imposed by restricting the study of music solely to private studios and the inspiration elicited from great composers, teachers, and conductors. The prac-

---

[1] The concept of "either-or" permeates the text. In scientific research, it is imperative that the student distinguish between factors that are separate and/or dependent. This concept will become more understandable as the student progresses through the text.

PART
ONE

aware of the vast possibilities of experimental research. New ways are constantly being found to shorten the time it takes to master notation, improve intonation, and increase perception and discrimination, to name but a few of the myriad topics under investigation.

For example, experiments in the area of intonation demonstrate a misleading aspect of strictly personal evaluation. A teacher may believe that a student has a tendency to sing out of tune in a specific situation and may tell him to remedy this tendency. The intonational deviation may be just the opposite of that observed by the teacher, but calling attention to intonation changes the performance regardless of what is said about the direction of the deviation.[2] The teacher may associate improved intonation with his definition of the intonational difficulty and believes that his definition was correct. He does not realize that perhaps *anything* he might have said about intonation would probably have influenced the performance. The teacher may then espouse the generality that students tend to go out of tune in a particular situation. If he is particularly influential, some faction of the music profession may incorporate an "absolute principle." This information combines with other "absolute principles," which are often antithetical, and helps contribute to the "great debates" in music. If the teacher were to test the effects of verbal conditioning upon intonation (using a well-constructed design with adequate controls), then the findings could contribute in a more positive manner to future performances.[3] This knowledge would provide a greater contribution to the profession. It would seem that experimental research holds potential benefits for every music instructor as an augmentation to present teaching effectiveness.

SCIENTIFIC APPLICATION

Music has had practical application for centuries. Literature abounds with examples of the use of music from the earliest times of man to the present.[4] It is apparent that music in various forms and patterns

---

[2] Clifford K. Madsen, "The Effect of Scale Direction on Pitch Acuity in Solo Vocal Performance," *Journal of Research in Music Education*, XIV, No. 4 (Winter, 1966).

[3] Donald G. Albert, "The Effect of Differential Rehearsal Techniques on Pitch Acuity," (Master's thesis, Florida State University, August, 1967).

[4] *See* Doris Soibelman, *Therapeutic and Industrial Uses of Music* (New York: Columbia University Press, 1948). E. Thayer Gaston, ed., *Music in Therapy* (New York: The Macmillan Company, 1968). D. M. Schullian and M. Schoen, eds., *Music and Medicine* (New York: Henry Schumann, Inc., 1948). *Music Therapy*, 1951–62 yearbooks of the NAMT (Lawrence, Kansas: The Allen Press). *Journal of Music Therapy* (Lawrence, Kansas: The Allen Press).

bring methodology and artistic attitude more into the twentieth century. This does not imply that Leopold Mozart was not a good instructor for young Wolfgang; he obviously was. It does seem unfortunate, however, that some applied musicians continue *not* to recognize anything outside of "apprenticeship" in the study of applied music, and most aspiring musicians are not Mozarts. Many problems encountered in learning performance skills can be studied scientifically. Does differential music training produce recognizably different results? What should be the optimum temporal relationship between individual, group, apprenticed, or other modes of music instruction? What can programmed instruction, aural, visual, tactile, or combinations of these and other stimuli contribute to music learning? Can psycho-motor skills be increased by extrinsic physiological manipulation before physical patterns are established? Is there a relationship between specific isometric-isotonic exercises and musical performance? What are the effects of various presentations of music literature and/or methodology on student motivation? It would seem that while expertise in teaching is invaluable, it need not be exclusive.

Musicians in institutions of higher learning to whom the responsibility of formal music study has been entrusted have consistently moved toward greater objectification in the instruction of music. The entire history of music education represents a dynamic expansion of music opportunities and improved methodology for increased numbers of students. However, the general tenor of even some of the best institutions still evidences great pressures from the past: the tacit assumption prevails that the best, if not the only, way to study music is to apprentice with a master. This attitude in its *extreme* seems to be based on three assumptions: (1) rejection of another teacher's worth, (2) religious dedication to one's one abstract ideas and methods (which possibly would change if tested experimentally), and (3) a firm belief that any student who does not produce from this inspired teaching is obviously untalented.

Certainly, the above attitudes are extreme and should find little expression in modern institutions. A narrow traditional approach to teaching leaves much to be desired, and often the simplest facts are overlooked. While many musicians spend their lives teaching neuro-muscular skills, some do not attempt to gain an understanding of basic physiology. For instance, many musicians teach their own particular concept of "diaphragmatic breathing" without having a firm knowledge of the human anatomy. This is just one area where extant misconceptions are perpetuated by well-meaning teachers of music who rely on traditional approaches rather than objective evidence. Therefore, many ideas and techniques that can be studied scientifically are still debated, espoused, and indoctrinated by various factions of the teaching profession. On the other hand, researchers within universities are becoming increasingly has been employed extensively as therapy in most cultures from their inception. Traditionally, music has often been associated with the supernatural. Some present-day writing still attests to this mystical illusion with citations from literature sources portraying the idea that music somehow finds its way into man's "soul" and serves to alleviate and ameliorate his physiological and psychological discomforts.[5] Nevertheless, scientific uses of music are becoming increasingly apparent.

During World War II, a discipline arose that has gained progressive scientific respectability. As the discipline evolved, the National Association for Music Therapy was founded (1950). The NAMT proposes to provide increasing application and research concerning music in therapy. Many mental hospitals presently employ music therapists who represent firm academic backgrounds in music and psychology. Registered music therapists are also employed in other diverse institutional and community settings, and the massive growth of the field would seem to attest to the validity of this embryonic, yet potentially powerful, specialty.[6]

Scientific application of music in therapy demands an objectivity that many musicians are not prepared to accept. The following are typical questions asked by a person who has just heard about the field: "Does music really help make people well?" "Is it really good for people?" The scientist (and, hopefully, the well-trained music therapist) has three possible answers once these questions are more specifically defined—Yes, No, or I don't know. His answer must be based on evidence, not conjecture. If some aspect of music is "good" for someone, then the scientist wants to know if it is also "bad." Specificity is the key. What specific music experience for what specific person in what specific situation, are factors that need to be known. That "patient X participated in the hospital chorus and seemed to enjoy it," has little meaning *per se* for the scientist. Experiments that test the effects of specified music and music activities in the reduction of specific maladaptive behaviors have greater meaning.[7] Also, the scientist may want to test the pejorative as well as the ameliorative effects of music.

The traditional music therapy training programs are associated with

---

5 Bessie R. Swanson, *Music in the Education of Children* (2nd ed., Belmont, Calif.: Wadsworth Publishing Company, Inc., 1964), pp. 1–2.

6 Registration is based upon an established curriculum, which includes a clinical internship of six months. Information concerning music therapy may be obtained by writing to the National Association for Music Therapy, P.O. Box 610, Lawrence, Kansas, 66044.

7 *See* B. H. Barrett, "Reduction in Rate of Multiple Tics by Free Operant Consequences," in *Case Studies in Behavior Modification,* eds. Leonard P. Ullmann and Leonard Krasner (New York: Holt, Rinehart & Winston, Inc., 1965), pp. ˜–63. Clifford K. Madsen *et al.,* "A Behavioral Approach to Music Therapy," *al of Music Therapy,* V, No. 3 (September, 1968).

schools of music and evidence pressures toward aesthetic fulfillment.[8] The music therapist generally has strong attitudes about music as a special *positive* force. However, it seems unwise for the practicing therapist to consider himself a music therapist, music educator, applied musician, conductor, and aesthetician all at the same time and at the same level of competency. The research therapist should be primarily concerned with testing the scientific application of music in therapy. Initial discrimination of role definition seems imperative for scientific objectification. Principles which fail to consider that music experiences used as therapy may often be entirely different from music used in other activities will be principles which are vague and non-utilitarian. As music therapy continues to develop into a behavioral science, it must be based on scientific principles demonstrated through research.

CONCLUSION

We live in a nation where research is of prime importance and where constant scientific investigation is being applied to almost all areas of endeavor. Today, children in grade school amaze their elders with new ways of learning mathematics, language proficiencies, and sophisticated facts from the social and physical sciences. All areas of music are proselyting these students in a highly competitive society. The perpetuation of excellent musical performance still demands many years of rigorous practice, as well as the best possible instruction. Music therapy evidences a progressive need to find new and more effective means of ameliorating man's illnesses, and music education has been entrusted with providing research benefits for the entire academic and general public communities. The music profession should dismiss personal prejudices, avail itself of all possible knowledge, support investigation that could prove beneficial, and work in concert to stimulate and evaluate new techniques and materials that can be produced from experimental research.[9]

STUDY QUESTIONS

1. Are there limitations to viewing the study of music as strictly *either* a science *or* an art? Explain.

---

[8] Clifford K. Madsen, "A New Music Therapy Curriculum," *Journal of Mus Therapy*, II, No. 3 (September, 1965).

[9] Parts of this chapter were initially presented in an article, "Experiment search in Applied Music," by Clifford K. Madsen, *Music Educators Jou* No. 6 (June–July, 1965).

2. What are three aspects of the scientific attitude, and how are they useful in the study of music?

3. As music therapy continues to develop into a behavioral science, it must be based on scientific principles demonstrated through research. Explain.

4. Assuming more musicians are being graduated from colleges and universities each year and the performance and abilities of these musicians are steadily improving, is research in the area of music education warranted? Explain.

5. Is it possible that music subjected to research could lose its impact as an art? Why?

CHAPTER TWO

methods of research in music

Although the focus of this text is primarily on experimental research, other modes of inquiry are presented to delineate the experimental area. There are four general methods of research in music: (1) philosophical, (2) historical, (3) descriptive, and (4) experimental. It should be stressed that all modes of inquiry may contribute significantly to knowledge. There are those who argue for one mode of investigation perhaps without realizing the varieties of individual issues, physical phenomena, and life experiences. It appears exceedingly narrow to give credence to only one mode of investigation. Certainly, all forms of research are appropriate for the music scholar.

THE PHILOSOPHICAL METHOD

The word philosophy elicits various responses from musicians. Often, it is considered in relation to the most important issues regarding all aspects of music, and conversely, it is sometimes used to refer to ideas and procedures that are "not practical." One often hears the phrase, "I don't have time to think about it, I have too much to do." Those who contrast "philosophical" and "practical" show their lack of understand ing. Whether something is "practical" or not is a legitimate question, but only in relationship to other factors that need explicit definition. Terminology that defines "practical" needs to be established before the question can be discussed and issues analyzed. This process of analysis and criticism, then, represents philosophical inquiry.

It would appear that all aspects of music activities need to be logically analyzed and criticized, to be thought and rethought. The foremost question of "Why?" concerning all music activities needs constant investigation. Thoughtful speculation should always precede important decisions. If this is not the case, there will be much foolish research. Richard Colwell states in the *Journal of Research in Music Education:* "It is the responsibility of philosophy to point the direction for research; to identify specific problems; to agree upon meanings of terms and upon both areas and levels of achievement; to locate and give voice to the needs of the profession so that research is done which can be truly beneficial." [1] Important relationships between "what is" and "what ought to be" merit extremely serious appraisal, as does the entire area of knowledge and how one knows anything. There is no substitute for coming directly or vicariously in contact with the most important ideas and positions available. To think without acting may result in loss, but to act without thinking may produce far worse consequences. *Analysis, criticism,* and *speculation* concerning all variables involved in music are imperative.

Analysis refers to searching out implications of assertions, their consistency, and the assumptions involved in a body of theory. Most research topics in music theory may be classified in the analysis category, for example, "Theoretical Analysis of Brahms' Alto Rhapsody." Additionally, music education concepts, techniques, and programs of study all need to be analyzed. *Criticism* refers to precise examination and evaluation of alternatives regarding musical procedures, compositions, or activities. Often, musical works are contrasted by period, composer, or style. Educational theories are sometimes criticized, for example, "The Impact of Montessori on Contemporary Music Education." Many times specific activities relating to interpretation of musical performance are criticized, for example, "Evaluation of Bel Canto Technique." *Speculation* concerns investigation into any aspect of music with a goal toward projections for the future. Most theories regarding aesthetics, art, intuition, music appreciation, attitudes, and values are speculations. It should be noted that many philosophical studies combine all three of

---

[1] Richard Colwell, "Music Education and Experimental Research," *Journal of Research in Music Education,* XV, No. 1 (Spring, 1967).

the above procedures in various proportions. Within a historical perspective, musicology is generally considered as the bridge between the philosophical and historical areas and most often involves analysis, criticism, and speculation.

THE HISTORICAL METHOD

The benefits derived from historical research should be obvious. Various forms of historical documentation are necessary if man is to transmit, other than by the spoken word, ideas and artifacts to future generations. Granted that historical evaluation has a bias, that is, it is most often written or perceived by the person in control, may not factually describe a "true event," and contains different "meaning" for everyone, the foremost question remains—what are the alternatives?

Perhaps one of the most unfortunate circumstances concerning man's interpersonal relationships arises from his seeming inability to learn from the past. While records from the past have provided one vehicle enabling technology to develop tremendously, historical documentation has not yet provided much improvement in man's ability to get along with himself and his fellowman (with or without music). A music teacher who would abhor subjecting his students to the physical discomforts he experienced as a child may calmly watch these same pupils suffer detrimental interpersonal relationships within the music ensemble, stating that "each person has to learn for himself." Thus, interpersonal problems seem to remain cyclic for each generation. Hopefully, those engaged in any aspect of historical research, even concerning the coldest facts, will somehow manage to elicit a spark of humanism that will help man *learn* from the past. This would seem especially pertinent in a "humanistic" area such as music.

Historical research in music is valuable in (1) analyzing the past; (2) preserving artifacts (for example, musical manuscripts, instruments); (3) discovering new artifacts; and (4) providing historical information from one specific situation for possible generalization to other areas. Rigorous historical documentation, even if thought to be deservedly inconspicuous, may help stimulate a respect for scholarship. Indeed, if any research project provides this experience, it is worthwhile.

THE DESCRIPTIVE METHOD

Descriptive methods of research enjoy great popularity, especially among researchers within universities. The most common descriptive method is the *survey*, which is based on one extremely simple premise—"If you want to know something about a person or a situation, ask." This method of investigation allows the collection of extensive amounts of information with the grestest economy of time. *Ex post facto* evaluation and analysis provide valuable information for interpretation for future action and data useful for *just knowing*. What are a person's musical values? How much money is spent on music activities in a certain city? How many music activities are there in a particular mental hospital? What do former students state as being most beneficial in their curriculum for professional development? From what socio-economic backgrounds do professional musicians come? Many diverse questions can be studied through survey techniques.[2]

Some problems encountered by the survey method should be stated. It would appear that a major drawback is a lack of reciprocity, especially when ascertaining opinions. Many questionnaires have never been returned because recipients felt that the questionnaire did not provide enough latitude in responses. The please-answer-yes-or-no direction that precedes many questionnaires (opinionnaires) discourages the thoughtful person. Even when the respondent has the option of five, eight, or ten gradations, *he may not like the questions*. Survey techniques that include some interaction, that is, interview techniques, help to rectify some of the objections but usually limit the number of respondents, therefore limiting the data. Nevertheless, many aspects of music and allied areas can benefit from survey methods. Survey methods include (1) studies of existing conditions, (2) comparisons of conditions, and (3) methods of improving conditions.

Interrelationship studies constitute a sub-class of the descriptive method and include (1) the case study, (2) causal comparative studies, and (3) correlational studies. The case study method enjoys extensive use, particularly in the fields of psychology and music therapy.[3] It recognizes the uniqueness of situations and circumstances and provides detailed information which usually concerns one subject. There is a growing number of researchers who reject the concept that group human behaviors or total music behavior involving many subjects can be studied collectively, combining actions and responses into "averages." Many behavioral psychologists categorically ignore any attempt to classify any aspect of group behaviors. These researchers may use extant statistical

---

[2] The survey is still perhaps the most popular method of research used in music education theses and dissertations. Excellent models for this type of research can be found in the *Journal of Research in Music Education*, MENC Publication, NEA Center; Washington, D.C.

[3] Examples of case studies can be found throughout professional literature. See Appendix A.

tools for evaluation, but it is usually in specific reference to repeated overt behavioral occurrences for each subject; therefore, the individual case study is preferred.[4]

Cases studíes may include total volumes devoted to unique patients or even biographies concerning great historical personages. Spitta's work on Bach [5] could certainly be classified as a major case history although this work is most often thought to be historical. The more frequent case studies generally contain information regarding persons neither as famous nor as rich in historical associations, for example, "A Case History of Five 'Dropouts' in a Public School Music Program." Some areas of investigation seem solely appropriate for the case study method where invaluable information is derived from this mode of research.

A second interrelationship method is the causal comparative study, which assesses causative factors by comparisons of different stimuli, subjects, or events. A third method is the correlational study, which does not assess causality but demonstrates significant relationships. (There may be a high correlation between drownings and ice cream sales, but most likely the drownings are not caused by the ice cream.)

Another sub-class of descriptive research is the *developmental study*. This mode of research concerns *growth* and *trend studies*. A growth study may assess the nature and rate of development of a program, an activity, groups, or individuals. A trend analysis is generally predictive and assesses specific aspects of development to clarify specific attributes and demonstrate significant differentiations. Trend and growth studies may be contrasted with historical research. While historical research deals with the past, a trend analysis describes the past in order to help predict the future, for example, "The Effect of Absolute Pitch Training Upon the Children of Schooled Musicians."

THE EXPERIMENTAL METHOD

Areas for experimental research are defined broadly to include any variable of interest for the music student who desires to use this particular methodology (see Chapters Three, Four, and Five). An experiment should be a most exact endeavor, characterized by the most stringent rigor. An experiment is designed to test a certain variable. This variable

---

4 See Werner K. Honig, *Operant Behavior: Areas of Research and Application* (New York: Appleton-Century-Crofts, 1966).

5 Philipp Spitta, *Johann Sebastian Bach, His Work and Influence on the Music of Germany (1685–1750)*, trans. Clara Bell and J. A. Fuller-Maitland (3 vols.; New York: Dover Publications, Inc., 1951).

must be isolated through definition or structure of a precise design and accurately measured insuring validity and reliability. An experiment is *valid* when it measures what it purports to measure. It is *reliable* when repeated measures yield similar results. The value of experimental research resides chiefly with the exactness of the specific knowledge that accrues from this mode of inquiry. Cause and effect relationships are established by isolating the experimental variable and manipulating certain other factors under highly controlled conditions to ascertain how and why a particular event occurs. The measurement of the variable depends upon precise independent manipulation. The *dependent variable* is measured data itself; the *independent variable(s)* are those controlled manipulations structured to produce the data.

Value judgments are both worthwhile and necessary, but a carefully designed experiment may provide far greater empirical evidence for causal relationships. Students may be aware of experimental research underlying the fields of medicine and the physical sciences, but the behavioral sciences and aesthetics have not been investigated through experimental manipulation to the degree evidenced in other areas. However, researchers have recently become increasingly aware of the value of experimentation within the behavioral sciences, and many areas of the humanities are also being quickly assimilated into the mainstream of scientific research.

The following chart represents different methods of investigation.

METHODS OF RESEARCH

I. Philosophical
    A. Analysis
    B. Criticism
    C. Speculation

II. Historical
    A. Documentary
    B. Artifacts

III. Descriptive
    A. Survey
        1. existing conditions
        2. comparisons of conditions
        3. method of improving conditions

    B. Interrelationship
        1. case study
        2. causal comparative study
        3. correlational study

C. Developmental
  1. growth study
  2. trend study
IV. Experimental
  A. One-sample
  B. Two-sample
  C. Multiple-sample

LIMITATIONS

A point of great confusion to most researchers concerns the differences between facts and value judgments. Some musicians argue value systems, sincerely believing they are arguing facts. In scientific research, a fact is a fact because it has monolithic acceptance or can be empirically verified. That Mozart wrote music is a fact; that Mozart's music is "good" is a value judgment. A value judgment can only be a value judgment if it is *not* a fact. There must be an equal possibility that Mozart's music is "bad" for it to be *judged* as "good." A fact is either-or, a value judgment is not.

Another major difficulty usually encountered by students who become interested in research is their inability to limit an idea to the point where it can be thoroughly investigated. The beginning researcher is sometimes discouraged by the realization that a major research endeavor provides only a minute and perhaps inconspicuous partial answer to a greater concern.

In experimental research, the importance of specificity, delimitation, and control cannot be overemphasized. A student may become tremendously excited about the effects of music on moods. After much work and time-consuming effort, he may arrive at an experimental design that attempts to test one overt physiological response to one sixteen-measure phrase. His previous enthusiasm may wane appreciably. His desire was to find what this great musical experience was all about; he wanted to see if it happened to everyone. With one study, he wanted to find the "answer" to the aesthetic experience. After the youthful fire is pinpointed to the precision of a laser beam, he may be left with an experiment that will take from three to six months to "test the effect of a selected sixteen-measure phrase on the pulse rate of fifty grade school musicians."

Unfortunately, many students yield to their original romantic desire and, encouraged by scientific naiveté, actually attempt to test everything simultaneously. Consequently, they may collect vast amounts of data that are useless. Often, a few "statistical tricks" are used to "beef up" the report, and then the report takes its place among similar studies that attempt to answer all questions and therefore answer none.[6] Possibly the worst result of this activity is the time serious researchers spend reviewing this morass, only to reject it because it lacks scientific control and precise investigation scrutiny.

CONCLUSION

There are many methods and techniques available for the researcher in music. All modes of inquiry are necessary and appropriate. Clear thinking and specificity are the keys to research. If the time spent in research is used wisely to illuminate important issues, describe and measure situations accurately, or test specific variables, the field of music will have many fragments of valid knowledge that collectively will provide focus for future action. The serious researcher should initially realize that he has indeed an "either-or" alternative concerning his first investigation. *Either* he can investigate a minute aspect of a larger problem and possibly arrive at clear significant information, *or* he can attempt to solve many problems, confound the issues, and add to extant conjecture.[7]

STUDY QUESTIONS

1. List the principal methods of research and briefly explain the value of each.
2. Why is "practical" inquiry important in music research?
3. Define "artifact" as related to historical research.
4. What are some problems of the survey method?
5. What are "either-or" alternatives with regard to experimental research?

---

[6] When the area of research interest is so large that it includes many diverse variables, experimental investigation should not be used unless issues can be defined; another mode of inquiry would be advisable.

[7] Organization of this chapter was based on a USOE project No. 6-1388, "A Conference on Research in Music Education," Henry L. Cady, Project Director, School of Music, The Ohio State University. Copies of this report may be obtained from ERIC Document Reproduction Center, Bell and Howell Co., 1700 Shaw Ave., Cleveland, Ohio 44112.

CHAPTER THREE

physical and perceptual bases for music experimentation

Music is organized sound and silence in time. Its two basic constituents are sound (pitch) and time (pitch and/or silence in spatial relationships, rhythm). These two aspects with ramifications involving people are the primary areas for experimental investigation. The four major areas of investigation for the researcher in music are: (1) physical bases of music, (2) perceptual bases of music, (3) psychological bases of music, and (4) pedagogical bases of music. A discussion of the physical (acoustical) and perceptual (physiological) aspects of music follows.

PITCH

Pitch refers to that subjective characteristic by which we differentiate musical frequencies. The term frequency, or *cycles per second*, is preferred by the physicists, because frequency is more exact than pitch and can be measured with existing equipment.[1] Recently, the term cps has been

---

[1] *See* Appendix D.

replaced by Hz after Heinrich Hertz, the late-nineteenth-century scientist who discovered radio waves. Noise varies from music, in that noise does not have *regular* vibrations (cps–Hz). Regular pulsations, from 1 to approximately 15 per second, are usually perceived as distinct, separate sounds (rhythm),[2] while separate impulses from 15–20 are perceived as pitch.[3] The lower limit of hearing pitch is thought to be approximately 20 Hz, the upper limit 20,000 Hz.[4] Pitch is judged by the listener and, as such, represents a socio-psychological phenomenon.[5] Pitch varies with loudness (intensity), quality (complexity), and duration, and also with the psychological and physiological disposition of the listener.

Myriad experiments regarding pitch have been conducted in fields outside the disciplines of music.[6] Precise equipment and a thorough knowledge of acoustics are necessary for sophisticated experimental research in physics. However, the researcher in music, with a tape recorder and/or a stroboscope can conduct many experiments on perception, discrimination, and reproduction of pitch.[7] Why do very young children seem to have such a highly developed sense of musical pitch compared to other auditory discriminations? Is "relative pitch" indeed relative only because of instruction? Would it be possible to teach extremely young children "absolute pitch" identifications much as they learn colors? Is "tone deafness" physiologically inherent or is it perhaps learned through modeling interior adult performances? Can pitch be used to enhance other auditory discriminations, such as phonics, words, or reading? What are the possibilities of pitch as stimulus control in eliciting or teaching other associations?

---

2 Frank A. Geldard, *The Human Senses* (New York: John Wiley & Sons, Inc., 1965), pp. 118–19. Carl E. Seashore, *The Psychology of Musical Talent* (Morristown, N.J.: Silver Burdett Company, 1919), p. 37.

3 Geldard, *op. cit.*, pp. 118–19. Seashore, *op. cit.*, p. 37. C.A. Taylor, *The Physics of Musical Sounds* (London: The English Universities Press, 1965), p. 148.

4 Charles A. Culver, *Musical Acoustics* (New York: McGraw-Hill Book Company, 1956), p. 65. Geldard, *op. cit.*, p. 95.

5 Paul R. Farnsworth, *The Social Psychology of Music* (New York: Dryden Press, 1958), p. 2.

6 Richard A. Campbell, "The Adequacy of a Traditional Place in the Perception of Periodicity Pitch" (Doctoral dissertation, State University of Iowa, 1962). Raymond J. Christman, "A Study of Shifts in Phenomenal Pitch as a Result of Prolonged Monaural Stimulation" (Doctoral dissertation, The Ohio State University, 1952). Bruce D. Faulds, "The Perception of Pitch in Music" (Doctoral dissertation, Princeton University, 1952). G. B. Henning, "The Effect of 'Aural Harmonics' on Frequency Discrimination," *Journal of the Acoustical Society of America*, XXXVII (1965), 1144–46. A. E. Rowenbeug, "The Effect of Masking Pitch of Periodic Pulses," *Journal of the Acoustical Society of America*, XXXVIII (1965), 747–58.

7 Appendix D.

QUALITY

Each transmitting source has its own unique quality. Each voice is different, musical instruments certainly produce different qualities, and even lawn mowers and car engines have distinguishing characteristics. Quality is that characteristic which differentiates sounds having similar pitch and loudness. The acoustical term for quality (timbre) is *complexity*.

Every musical sound is composed not only of its major distinguishing characteristics (for example, A = 440 Hz), but also of other sounds heard simultaneously. These other sounds are called *overtones* or *partials*. A trumpet tone perceived as a concert C contains not only the frequency necessary for that particular C, but other frequencies whose unique arrangement gives the trumpet its characteristic quality. The amount and relative intensity of the other parts of the trumpet sound make it possible (for most people) to distinguish it from an oboe, violin, or piano.[8]

It is assumed that all musicians are familiar with the "overtone series" or the partials, which in many instances are derived from exact mathematical multiples of the fundamental.

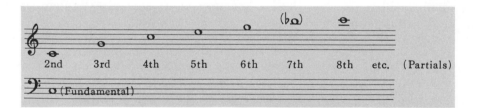

FUNDAMENTAL AND PARTIALS

A pure tone, if indeed it exists, consists of one frequency. A complex tone usually consists of a fundamental (the lowest frequency) and certain other specific frequencies which, when combined, provide distinguishing characteristics referred to as quality.

Many differences in quality that can be detected by electronic equipment escape human differentiation.[9] While extensive laboratory equipment is essential in the investigation of precise tonal analysis, many

---

[8] Culver, *Musical Acoustics*, p. 105. Alexander Wood, *The Physics of Music* (London: Methuen and Co., 1950), pp. 70–77.

[9] J. C. Rissit, "Computer Study of Trumpet Tones," *Journal of the Acoustical Society of America*, XXXVIII, No. 6 (1965), p. 912.

experiments can be conducted empirically to ascertain just what differences in quality are detected by musicians. Previous experimentation in this area demonstrates that, quite often, musicians cannot hear certain differences they believe exist and, conversely, often seem to "hear" much more than can be measured electronically.[10] This seems to be particularly evident in reference to expensive or old instruments or in justification of a certain methodology.

The composite effects of different qualities also need investigation. What sounds are associated with other sensory experiences? What would be the effect on presently constituted musical ensembles of expanding or modifying quality through electronic instrumentation? Is there a "cultural predisposition" toward certain musical qualities? Can pitch and/or quality be used as musical stimuli to effect other behaviors, such as improved speech or hearing?

LOUDNESS

Loudness or intensity is perhaps the most obvious characteristic of sound and warrants extensive experimentation. Intensity is of vital concern to industry, the medical profession, conductors, marching bands, and apparently to many small combos who seem to work on the premise that "If the volume doesn't hurt, forget it."

Some of the questions to be asked in experimentation are these: What intensity is necessary to command attention in music listening? What is the relationship between an original intensity level and selected reproduction levels of the same musical performance? What are the precise intensity levels of individual performers or sections when a musical group is "balanced"? What are the effects of loudness on emotional behaviors? What are the effects of differing noise levels in relationship to learning?

Pitch is to some extent influenced by loudness and should always be controlled in any experimental manipulation.[11] Experimentation could be done on the effects of loudness in relationship to all other musical ingredients. Loudness is measured in decibels (db) and equipment for objective measurement is not exorbitantly expensive (see Appendix D).

DURATION

Duration of sound is often one of the most overlooked and yet vital aspects of music. Experimentation concerning duration of individual

---

10 Farnsworth, *The Social Psychology of Music*, pp. 9–10.

11 Culver, *Musical Acoustics*, p. 84. Geldard, *The Human Senses*, p. 122.

pitches has been conducted,[12] but little investigation has involved the temporal-spatial elements of successive pitches (rhythm). This dearth of research may be caused by the lack of inexpensive precise instruments that can measure rhythmic responses. The development of the Conn Chromatic Stroboscope (Stroboconn) stimulated a great amount of research, probably because of the ease with which individual *pitch* deviations could be measured, but there have not been many investigations concerning rhythm. The several research reports on precise rhythm measurement used specific apparatus usually designed especially for each experiment.[13] Kymograph (time line instruments used for measurements of heart patterns (EKG), of brain waves (EEG), and of muscle potential (EMG) have been available for some time, although many researchers seem reluctant to adapt their use to the measurement of performed rhythms. The development of an *inexpensive* measuring device capable of precise measurement of temporal-spatial impulses should have great heuristic value as a research tool in music experimentation.[14]

Many experiments can be conducted with simple and inexpensive equipment such as an accurate electric metronome, Standard timer (electric clock), and so on. These experiments would not allow the measurement of individual notes, but could establish total temporal deviation over selected rhythm patterns or other variables involving sound in time.

It would appear that consequential contributions to the study of rhythm will initially be those concerned with rhythm in relationship to the physiological limitations and psychological perceptions evidenced in rhythmic "internalization" and rhythmic reproduction (performance). Clichés such as "read ahead" and "sub-divide the beat" might achieve greater meaning when researchers find answers to some basic questions. What is the limit of man's temporal evaluation? (Man obviously cannot tell time as evidenced by the chronoscopes he straps to his arms.) What is a beat? How is a beat measured in music? How slow can a beat occur and still be a beat? How fast? Is all music actually organized or based upon beats, meters, and rhythms? How should beats be sub-divided? Why is the division of twos and multiples of twos (simple) so different

---

12 C. D. Creelman, "Human Discrimination of Auditory Duration" (Doctoral dissertation, University of Michigan, 1961). K. Danziger, "Effect of Variable Stimulus Intensity on Estimates of Duration," *Perceptual and Motor Skills*, XX (1965), 505–508.

13 *See* Bernard Linger, "An Experimental Study of Durational Notation" (Doctoral disseration, Florida State University, 1966). Alan H. Drake, "An Experimental Study of Selected Variables in the Performance of Musical Durational Notation," *Journal of Research in Music Education*, XVI, No. 4 (Winter, 1968), 329–38.

14 S. Fleming, "The Beats Have Found A Master (Tempometer)," *High Fidelity*, XV (April, 1961), 28.

from that of three (compound)? Is it possible for one to sub-divide anything larger than a division of four to *one* beat?[15] What constitutes a scientific definition of rubato and style? How long should a pitch be held within a specific musical context? What determines neuromuscular responses to different temporal stimuli? Why? These are but a few of the many questions open to investigation.

PERCEPTION

Perception of sound has been a subject of serious concern to many diverse investigators representing various disciplines.[16] The ability to hear seems of extreme consequence to everyone in general and to musicians in particular. It is obvious that music must be perceived to exist (with the possible exception of notation, which also necessitates prior hearing if the symbols are to have much meaning).

Researchers in the fields of medicine, physiology, and communication have provided most of the existing knowledge of pitch perception and hearing discrimination.[17] If the perception of minute musical pitch differentiations were as vital to man as his ability to recover a hearing loss, communicate with a loved one, or listen to a ball game, then music researchers would probably become more involved with the perception of sound. Since it is assumed that "everyone can hear music," this pursuit lacks the concern expressed in other fields. There are many questions that may not only prove interesting, but also, when answered, substantially revise current practices regarding music performance, therapy, and education. Preferences in quality, loudness, and certain orchestrations may be solely extensions of physiological perceptual limitations.

---

[15] Lewis Pankaskie, "Rudiments of Rhythm," Florida State University, Tallahassee, Florida, 1965.

[16] H. G. Birch, I. Belmont, and E. Karp, "Social Differences in Auditory Perception," *Perceptual and Motor Skills*, XX (1965), 861–70. A. E. Brown, "Measurement of Auditory Thresholds," *Journal of the Acoustical Society of America*, XXXVIII (1965), 86–92. G. A. Gescheider, "Resolving of Successive Clicks by the Ears and Skin," *Journal of Experimental Psychology*, LXXI (1966), 378–81. R. G. Petzold, "The Development of Auditory Perception of Musical Sounds by Children in the First Six Grades," *Journal of Research in Music Education*, XI (1963), 21–43.

[17] H. Davis, "Peripheral Coding of Auditory Information," *Sensory Communication* (Cambridge, Mass.: The M.I.T. Press, 1961), pp. 119–41. J. D. Harris, "Loudness Discrimination," *Journal of Speech and Hearing Disorders*, Monograph Supplement, No. 11. G. B. Henning, "Frequency Discrimination of Random Amplitude Tones," *Journal of the Acoustical Society of America*, XXXIX (1966), 336–39. W. D. Neff, "Neural Mechanisms of Auditory Discrimination," *Sensory Communication* (Cambridge, Mass.: The M.I.T. Press, 1961), pp. 259–78.

Musical taste as well as performance difficulties encountered with specific instruments may be directly related to perception.

Experiments testing aural differentiation variables are appropriate topics for investigation. Are there perceptible differences among various brands of instruments? Between the C and D trumpets? Among various models of the same instruments? Between old and new violins? Differentially-priced pianos? Similar melodies? Scale constructs? Different musical styles? Various keys? Many similar questions have indeed been investigated, but there are endless possibilities that remain for the experimental researcher in music.

PHYSIOLOGICAL EFFECTS

The presence of a "deaf" person at a concert, the use of music as an inhibitor of pain, or the conduction of sound through diverse anatomical media attests to the knowledge that music can be felt as well as heard.[18] Perhaps the strong "internalization of the beat" evidenced in dancing and deemed necessary for most musical performance is but another indication that music elicits other tactile responsiveness in addition to the hearing process.

It has been demonstrated that music has the power to modify, to some extent, many physiological processes. Experiments in changes in pulse rate, blood pressure, and respiration as well as "mood" changes measured subjectively and objectively have been reported continuously from as early as 1897.[19]

The subjectivity, inadequate control, and lack of precise measuring instruments cause many of the early investigations to be suspect.[20] The development, both quantitative and qualitative, of precise measuring devices promises expanded research in the physiological area.[21] Also, current bio-chemical research demonstrates physiological changes in behavior that may soon be commonplace in therapy and education.[22] It is

---

[18] Clifford K. Madsen, *et al.*, "The Effect of Sound on the Tactile Threshold of Deaf Subjects," *Journal of Music Therapy*, II, No. 2 (June, 1965), 64–68.

[19] Douglas S. Ellis and Gilbert Brighouse, "Effect of Music on Respiration and Heartbeat," *American Journal of Psychology*, LXV, No. 1 (1952), 39–47. Paul R. Farnsworth, "A Study of the Hevner Adjective List," *Journal of Aesthetics and Art Criticism*, XIII, No. 9 (1954), 97–103. Doris Soibelman, *Therapeutic and Industrial Uses of Music* (New York: Columbia University Press, 1948), pp. 21–81.

[20] *Ibid.*, pp. 21–22.

[21] Appendix D.

[22] Soibelman, *op. cit.*, pp. 82–83. Murray E. Jarvik, "The Psychopharmacological Revolution," *Psychology Today*, CRM Associates, Del Mar, California (May, 1967), pp. 51–59.

extremely difficult, if not impossible, to separate the physiological from the psychological effects of music. It *is* possible to measure overt responses to controlled stimuli to ascertain specific effects in a well-designed experiment. Investigations that report *overt* responses would seem to have greater meaning than speculative conjecture concerning inferred causes.

CONCLUSION

There has been substantial research on the subject of the physical (acoustical) bases of music, but there are many challenges for the researcher interested in pitch, quality, loudness, and duration aspects of sound. The processes of hearing music as well as the effects of music on physiological responses need continued investigation. Textbooks in music theory, fundamentals of music, music for elementary teachers, music appreciation, and so on, are produced in ever-increasing proportions without benefits of experimental research. It would seem that experimental studies could precede and augment current practices.

Again the "either-or" concept should be stressed. It should be apparent that the scientific experimenter can only *deal with the empirical world and measure that which is demonstrable*. The researcher should be content to investigate that which is verifiable and not confuse issues, events, or experiences. Perception and physiological effects are quite different from how one "feels." The world of music is not necessarily an "either-or"; but one does have to know when he is engaged in which mode of inquiry.

STUDY QUESTIONS

1. Define music and discuss its two basic constituents.
2. Compare a "pure tone" to a complex tone and briefly explain the overtone series.
3. List and discuss the four physical components of music.
4. Discuss the statement "Pitch is judged by the listener, and as such represents a psycho-sociological phenomenon." What factors could possibly change pitch perception?
5. List types of experiments that could be conducted dealing with each of the physical, perceptual, and physiological aspects of music.

CHAPTER FOUR

psychological bases for music experimentation

There are many psychological bases for experimental research, but several areas need clarification before the structure of an experiment can be considered. Specificity is still the key, and the researcher must define all issues in order to know precisely which musical variables are appropriate for experimental research.

LANGUAGE ASPECTS OF MUSIC

Music has often been called "a universal language." Whether or not music is indeed a language must depend upon definition. If one supposes reciprocal communication as a defining prerequisite for a language, then certainly music is not a language—much less universal. If one simply means that different types of "music" are evident universally and enjoyed by many, or that music is capable of eliciting differential responses, then music may qualify. The latter definition, however, distorts the concept of language as generally used and attests not to communicative aspects of music, but to the universal and/or specific enjoyment of different types of music. If reciprocity is *not* essential for communication (for example, a textbook where the student cannot ask the author questions), then music may constitute a "non-verbal form of communication." [1]

One basic problem regarding the language aspects of music concerns the intent of the composer. To ask, "What is the composer trying to say?" appears somewhat questionable, for the composer may not know what he is trying to "say" or what specific mood he is trying to create, or he may not be trying to "say" anything.[2] If music is a language, then what does it communicate? Specific words? Concepts? Ideations? Images? Moods? The definition of specific linguistic communication may certainly be stretched to include music, but to what avail? If exact linguistic symbolization is the goal, it would seem wise to leave communication to more accurate and specific models, that is, English, French, Serbo-Croatian, and instead study the effects of music as a "non-verbal form of communication." While music is often used in therapy as an initial contact designed to elicit responsiveness and provide a vehicle for increased verbal behavior,[3] this application of music should not be confused with verbal communication.

Experimentation in the area of learning theory shows that (1) if a person knows what he is supposed to do in a learning situation, (2) and he wants to do it, (3) he probably will.[4] It is possible to program specific associations to music stimuli (for example, the motifs of Wagner), and the indoctrinated musician will "know the correct associations." [5] These learned responses probably enhance the total aural musical experience and certainly are not detrimental. It should be emphasized, however, that specific indoctrinated responses are quite different from a nondescript elusive "power of communication."

There does seem to be justification for music as a powerful behavioral elicitor, especially in proportion to experiential reinforcement.[6] The researcher could possibly add credence to this concept through careful experimentation. Furthermore, the specific area of verbal texts

---

[1] E. Thayer Gaston, "Man and Music," in E. Thayer Gaston (Ed.), *Music in Therapy* (New York: The Macmillan Company, 1968), pp. 7–27. W. W. Sears, "Processes in Music Therapy," in E. Thayer Gaston, *Music in Therapy*, pp. 30–44.

[2] Paul R. Farnsworth, *The Social Psychology of Music* (New York: Dryden Press, 1958), p. 142.

[3] Farnsworth, *op. cit.*, pp. 259–60.

[4] Donald R. Peterson and Perry London, "Behavioral Treatment of A Child's Eliminative Disturbance," *Case Studies in Behavior Modification*, Eds. Leonard P. Ullmann and Leonard Krasner (New York: Holt, Rinehart, & Winston, Inc., 1965), p. 290.

[5] Farnsworth, *The Social Psychology of Music*, pp. 106, 111.

[6] Robert W. Lundin, *An Objective Psychology of Music*, 2nd ed. (New York: Ronald Press, 1967), pp. 172–77.

(for example, opera, art songs, musical comedy) also needs careful research to differentiate the singular and collective effects of text and music. "Communication" may be verified through controlled research when the *effects* of music training and the psychological emotional changes elicited from music and verbal stimuli (affects of music) demonstrate observable behavioral changes. An exact terminological classification needs to be developed to objectify this subjective area before experimentation can begin.

AFFECTS OF MUSIC

Several researchers have studied affective responses to music as evidenced from verbal reports. Lists of adjectives are constructed, music is played, and respondents indicate their "mood." [7] This research represents a commendable effort, but often places the subject in much the same situation as the composer or artist who is compelled to describe his work verbally. It should be considered that there is at least the possibility that artistic and verbal expressions of man may have very little to do with each other. It should also be considered that the questioning process may actually force a subject to conceptualize, visualize, and theorize, when if left alone, he would not. Northrop, in describing the differences between the oriental and occidental cultures gives a rationale for perception of art as "immediately apprehendable" as opposed to "theoretical." [8] The questions "How does it make you feel," "What meaning do you get out of it" are strangely reminiscent of some therapists who constantly interpolate motives in human behavior to justify the elaborate theories that perhaps exist only in their own minds. Nevertheless, there is certainly a great amount of evidence, both scientific and naively empirical, to indicate that music is capable of eliciting differential behavior. Verbal responses as expressions of mood affects need intensive investigation. Research possibilities in this area would seem of vital concern to the music therapist, especially concering "feedback" from patients in ascertaining therapeutic effectiveness.

---

[7] K. Hevner, "Expression in Music; A Discussion of Experimental Studies and Theories," *Psychological Review*, XLIV (1935), 186–204. K. Hevner, "Experimental Studies of the Elements of Expression in Music," *American Journal of Psychiatry*, XLVIII (1936), 246–68. M. Schoen and E. L. Gatewood, Chapters 7 and 8, *The Effects of Music*, Ed. M. Schoen (New York: Harcourt, Brace & World, Inc., 1927).

[8] F. S. C. Northrop, *The Meeting of East and West* (New York: The Macmillan Company, 1960). F. S. C. Northrop, *The Logic of the Sciences and Humanities* (New York: The Macmillan Company, 1948).

MUSICAL TASTE

Individual and collective musical taste have been investigated for years.[9] Unfortunately, most of the concern expressed about musical taste often appears to originate with musicians and educators who seem to be trying to "elevate" the taste of the general public. It also seems more than coincidental that many "researchers" are primarily preoccupied with that music which they believe represents the finest selectivity.[10] It would appear that most people "like" music that has been repeatedly experienced and that they are taught to "like" (that is, music that has been positively reinforced). However, there may be many individual differences of opinion concerning specific composers and individual works. Researchers have gathered vast amounts of data to support general and specific theories of sociological aspects of musical taste. Eminence rankings, enjoyment ratings, counting of recordings, knowledge of composers, space allocations, and program analysis represent areas of investigation.[11] It would appear that musical taste stems from some form of indoctrination in relationship to both social and individual factors. There seem to be pronounced cultural similarities as well as many individual differences.[12]

If there is, indeed, some philosophical justification for music selectiveness, or if there are architectonic justifications for music preferences, these also should be investigated. However, the appropriate mode of inquiry might not be experimental investigation. There seem to be two aspects of taste that may be studied objectively: (1) status quo studies to determine exactly what constitutes taste, and (2) experimental studies designed to test the effects of learning on taste. Both of these areas need terminological classification and objective sampling methods. The sociological area is generally well-suited to descriptive research; longitudinal studies where subjects or music experiences are manipulated or rotated over long periods of time may be investigated experimentally.

MUSICAL ABILITIES

Various researchers have developed myriad tests to evaluate *musical abilities,* for example, aptitude, appreciation, discrimination, perfor-

---

[9] John H. Mueller, "The Social Nature of Music Taste," *Journal of Research in Music Education,* IV, No. 2 (Fall, 1956), 120.

[10] Farnsworth, *The Social Psychology of Music,* p. 136.

[11] Farnsworth, *op. cit.,* pp. 116–77. Lundin, *An Objective Psychology of Music,* pp. 179–89.

[12] Farnsworth, *op. cit.,* pp. 152–53.

mance, and so on.[13] The early work of Seashore represents a significant contribution in this area.[14] Other researchers have developed the area in greater detail and specificity.[15] The tests, however, have not enjoyed the use and respect that many initially thought they would have. Many students probably go through music experiences, from elementary school through graduate study, without ever taking any of these tests. Perhaps, ways could be found to make better use of these instruments in the selection and evaluation of music experiences. However, there are those who question the purpose of any such testing and ask, "Why have such tests? How can they be used? Are the tests indeed productive in any way? [16] While extensive work has been done to test the tests and also to correlate them with other attributes, such as intelligence, socio-economic background, achievement,[17] and so on, much remains to be done in this area.

It would seem that the music researcher should also be concerned about the lack of valid and reliable live performance tests. The few rare exceptions in this void, for example, "Watkins-Farnum Performance Scale,"[18] provide the only assessment of actual performance. For some time it has been evident that paper and pencil studies provide only partial answers to performing variables. It is one thing to be able to discriminate subtle differences between two very similar tones; it is quite

---

[13] William E. Whybrew, *Measurement and Evaluation in Music* (Dubuque, Iowa: William C. Brown Co., 1962), pp. 6–7. Paul R. Lehman, *Tests and Measurements in Music* (Englewood Cliffs, N.J.: Prentice-Hall, Inc., 1968).

[14] Carl E. Seashore, *Psychology of Music* (New York: McGraw-Hill Book Company, 1938).

[15] Edwin Gordon, *Musical Aptitude Profile* (Boston: Houghton-Mifflin Company, 1965). H. D. Wing, "A Revision of the Wing Musical Aptitude Test," *Journal of Research in Music Education*, X (Spring, 1962), 39–46. Lehman, *Tests and Measurements in Music* (Englewood Cliffs, N.J.: Prentice-Hall, Inc., 1968).

[16] Whybrew, *op. cit.*, p. 5.

[17] Edward L. Rainbow, "A Pilot Study to Investigate the Constructs of Musical Aptitude," *Journal of Research in Music Education*, XIII, No. 1 (Spring, 1965), p. 3. Clarence E. Garder, "Characteristics of Outstanding High School Musicians," *Journal of Research in Music Education*, III (1955), 11–20. W. S. Graves, "Factors Associated with Children's Taking Music Lessons, Including Some Parent-Child Relationships," *Pedagogical Seminary*, LXX (1947), 65–125. Leta S. Hollingworth, "Music Sensitivity of Children Who Test Above 135 IQ," *Journal of Educational Psychology*, XVII (1962), 95–109, Jo Ann M. Hughes, "59 Case Studies of the Effect of Music Participation on Social Development," *Music Educators Journal*, XLI (February, 1954), 58–59. J. L. Mursell, *The Psychology of Music* (New York: W. W. Norton & Company, Inc., 1937). Hazel M. Stanton, "Measurement of Musical Talent: The Eastman Experiment," *University of Iowa Studies in the Psychology of Music*, II (1935), 1–140.

[18] J. G. Watkins and S. E. Farnum, *The Watkins-Farnum Performance Scale* (Winona, Mich.: Leonard Music, 1962).